Rabindranath and Gangadhar

Rabindranath and Gangadhar

Manindra Kumar Meher

Translated by
Malabika Patel

Black Eagle Books
USA address:
7464 Wisdom Lane
Dublin, OH 43016

India address:
E/312, Trident Galaxy, Kalinga Nagar,
Bhubaneswar-751003, Odisha, India

E-mail: info@blackeaglebooks.org
Website: www.blackeaglebooks.org

First International Edition Published by
Black Eagle Books, 2024

RABINDRANATH AND GANGADHAR
by **Manindra Kumar Meher**
Translated by **Malabika Patel**

Cover & Interior Design: Ezy's Publication

ISBN- 978-1-64560-570-6 (Paperback)

Printed in the United States of America

Prologue by the Author

Since my childhood I had been seeing two oil paintings on the wall of our ancestral house at Barapalli. One was of Swabhaba kabi Gangadhar Meher and the other of Viswakabi Rabindranath Tagore. Kabi Gangadhar Meher happened to be my great grandfather and it was therefore natural that an intimate belongingness would get imbibed in me. But surprisingly for Viswakabi, I did not sense any feeling of remoteness. I never enquired about the reason why my grandfather Bhagaban Meher, worthy son of Swabhaba Kabi Gangadhar Meher had ordered to hang the two pictures in close proximity. The picture of Rabindranath in his flowing gown while receiving the Nobel Prize had created a deep impact on me in my childhood. Another colour photo of his - taken while immersed in reading a book - that was hung in our study had also remained wedged in my memory. Since childhood this fondness that I developed for these two immortal souls would later develop into an all consuming veneration.

While celebrating Gangadhar Jayanti, many writers opine that if Gangadhar Meher's poetry could have been translated into English, he could have got a Nobel prize.

Whether it would have happened or not, that Gangadhar's poetic genius was marvellously divine, there are no two opinions. Some even go to the extent of lauding his poetry more than Rabindranath. For me however, both were on the same footing. Being inspired by the life philosophy of both the writers, I have expressed my adulation for them uniformly while making critical assessments of their literary works.

Both the poets create the same emotional stirrings in me. In the quiet evenings or in the silent hours of the night, in moments of solitude, I have enjoyed reciting Rabindranath's Geetanjali. Similarly whenever I am unwell physically or mentally, I have sung Gangadhar's poems till I have fallen asleep. The profound solace and peace I have derived from these recitations are indeed indescribable.

For a long time, I had been nurturing a desire to visit Shantiniketan. Finally in 1997 I got the opportunity - I was selected on behalf of Sahitya Akademi - to undertake a tour of Shantiniketan. Just as I used to feel at home – as the great grandson of Gangadhar – while visiting Barapalli - the birth place of Gangadhar - I got the same homely feeling while visiting Shantiniketan. Whether anybody would believe or not, I felt I too am the great grandson of Rabindranath. After that I got many an opportunity to visit Shantiniketan which I would love to believe were the doings of the invisible hands of the great poet. Further, in the portrait of Rabindranath in Shatiniketan, I could mentally perceive the picture of Gangadhar and in the portrait of Gangadhar in Barapalli, I could catch a glimpse of Rabindarnath. For me, both the icons were hardly distinguishable.

Making a comparative study on both the great poets then became a strong urge in me. I tried my hand in writing a few articles. After that, the idea of publishing it in a book form got hold of me. While studying and analyzing their works both in Bengali and Odia, I never felt who is superior or inferior of the two, but how equally inspiring both the poets are by delving deep into their souls.

I am sincerely grateful to Shri Satya Patnaik, founder of Black Eagle Publications for publishing this book on comparative literature. For my loving students who took pains to type it out in Odia, they have my blessings galore. Shri Madhabanada Patra, Darpadalan Rath, Dr, Sridhar Barik, Rakesh Barik have been a source of strength and support. If this book adds to the study of comparative literature, my efforts would find its own reward.

Manindra Kumar Meher
July 2022

Translator's Note

On a morning of November 2023, I received the Odia book 'Rabindranath O Gangadhar', couriered and signed by the author Manindra kumar Meher with a request to translate it into English. Two days later I was to be wheeled into the OT of a hospital for a major surgery. My instant thought to the author's request was, I can, only if I survive this ordeal, Lord Jagannath willing.

The surgery was successful but it took me five months to be on my feet. As promised to the Lord, I started reading the book. It is common knowledge that Rabindranath Tagore, the single Nobel Laureate in literature that India has produced is also Bengal's greatest writer ever. He is nonpareil, internationally acclaimed and greater than all the writers of India put together. Gangadhar Meher is Odisha's celebrated and popular poet, but confined to Odisha. Can there be any comparison between the two? One was born into a privileged background with a silver spoon in his mouth while another was born into a weaver's family and had to struggle for earning his livelihood. So where was the likeness?

As I started leafing through the book, I discovered the uncanny similarities between the two great lives and their literary sensibilities as expounded by the author. It was a revelation to me, hailing from a non-literature background, as it were. Many readers like me, I felt, would not have perceived such a parallel between the two great writers. To the English readers and literary critics, therefore, such content would be a value addition; was my gut feeling, before I embarked on the job of translating the book.

I started translating a page per day, acutely aware that the lyrical and at place ornamental Odia language of the author is being lost in translation. Professor Meher's Odia is exquisite, his choice of words unique, for which it was difficult to find the right English equivalent. As regards the citations, Rabindranath's poems have been widely translated, so there were no problems in fetching them. For the English translation of Gangadhar Meher's poems, I resorted to 'Gangadhar Meher: Selected works' by the indubitable Jayanta Mahapatra and Madhusudan Pati. The voluminous book; an omnibus of Gangadhar's oeuvre took my breath away. On the sidelines, I may say, it is a must read for any lover of literature.

My thanks are due to Professor Meher for reposing the faith in me to translate the book and to the Publishers; Black Eagle books for publishing the same. If the English translation benefits the students of comparative literature and English readers, my labour would find its reward.

Malabika Patel
August 2024

Contents

Prologue 5

Translator's Note 9

A Stanza from Tapaswini and a Poem from Geetanjali 13

Wives of Rabindranath and Gangadhar: Mrinalini and Shanta Devi 20

The first poem of Geetanjali and Bharasa poem of Gangadhar 26

Sons: Shamindra and Arjun 30

Poems: Bangamata and Matrubhumi 37

Protests against British Rule 43

Shantiniketan and Barapalli 48

Two Prayer Poems 52

Invoking the Divine and celebrating Amrut 57

Fighting Adversity 61

Study in ideation 65

Drishtidan and Tapaswini 69

Two Ideal sons 74

Views on Education 78

A Stanza from Tapaswini and a Poem from Geetanjali

Discerning readers can judge the way life-philosophy of a poet is reflected in his poems. Poem Tapaswini is the masterpiece of Swabhaba kabi Gangadhar Meher. He had not penned his life story. But his creation Tapaswini can be said to be the story of his soul realization. Be it depiction of a character, or description of nature, in all through his craft of poignant tales, his heartbeat can be heard in a very subtle way. It lies not in the plot or storyline, but in the inner musings of the poet. Those readers who immerse themselves fully in his outpourings of words can sense the poets' inner churning. That Tapaswini, the tour de force of the poet richly deserves a special study, need not be emphasized. In this essay we focus on one stanza of his poem Tapaswini.

The fourth canto of Tapaswini is *'Mangale Aela Usha'* which is set to Raag chokhi. In this canto the main character Sita, is said to be residing with the maidens of a hermitage in the banks of Tamasa River. Her stay in such a secluded place is described in a manner which oozes with a radiant life force. Tamasa, may be a river but it is described as a living soul. Murmuring, rippling, the river flows away to a faraway land. And in her bubbling flow the music of her soul reverberates. Not all can hear the music. Only the pure heart, Sita, the daughter of Mother Earth can hear the melody of the gurgling river waves. Gangadhar has captured that music of the river, which no other Ramayan literature has ever done. After caressing Sita, river Tamasa is suffused with a divine delight, which is described by the poet as incomparable. As if, the river was waiting since time immemorial to share her life experience with Sita. What all has she not said? Instead of going into all that it would suffice to quote one stanza in which the river's heartbeat has been expressed in an exquisite manner. The famous stanza, that effectively captures the poetic exuberance of Gangadhar is reproduced:

[1]*Meandering through many forests,*
Unbeguiled in charming canyons
Crossing numerous obstacles with a clear vision
Not counting the pain of darkness, nor charmed
By the joy of light, I keep to my long course
With deep bowed head, so I fulfill my life
Pleasing with gifts of water all who live on my banks.

The life philosophy of river Tamasa, as if resonates with the detached karma espoused in Bhagabat Gita. Tamasa keeps flowing in her endless journey, crossing so many hazards on the way, navigating the highs and lows, overcoming the perilous paths, but flows on steadfastly towards her ultimate destination. Her entire voyage is a journey in purity and chastity. She doesn't consider

1 Translation by Jayanta Mahapatra & Madhusudan Pati, Gangadhar Meher Selected Works, Ed. Madhusudan Pati, Sambalpur University&Aryan Books International 2001. p34

darkness as her pain or luminosity as her pleasure. With humility she keeps giving away her treasure to the needy with nary an expectation. Rather she imbues it with her pure love. The words in the stanza reflect the soul realization of the poet. As if, spontaneously, the poet expresses his innermost feelings through the ponderings of the river. Poet Gangadhar's entire life was like the river Tamasa, devoted and completely dedicated to the Almighty. Without anything in return, river Tamasha had dedicated her every moment in the service of her land and its people. Such a desire-free life can be said to be a liberated life in the words of Buddha. Similarly going beyond the worldly cares and transcending the pains and pleasures of human existence, the poet, Gangadhar had devoted his life in spreading joy to others. A poet's pen - whether it serenades a river or a woman, the terrain or a bird, the trees or the animals – vibrates with the pulse of life. From this angle the stanza reflects the poet's self-rumination and touches the heart of the discerning reader.

Viswakabi Rabindranath was also a wordsmith of similar feelings. 'Geetanjali' is nothing but his soul's offering. Inspired by the Upanishadic contemplation it can make the readers' heart-strings quiver forever, as it contains the highest vibrations of an enlightened soul. In many couplets of Geetanjali, such heavenly sensibilities can be felt.

However, in the present context, one poem of Viswakabi has been chosen as an instance. The famous writer of Odisha, Shri Haraprasad Das has rendered an exquisite Odia translation of the English version of Geetanjali. Writer Shri Das has admitted to being overwhelmed while translating Geetanjali and has eulogized the divine sensibilities of Viswakabi in each of his poems. Every translator worth his salt is said to have waxed lyrical while transcreating the immortal creations of the Nobel Laureate. Here we quote one of his poems (number 12 of Geetanjali), the essence of which is: the poet goes round the universe in search of his God, knocks at every door, gets exhausted and finally when he closes his eyes and immerses himself in his innermost shrine, he can see his God.

> [2]*The time that my journey takes is long*
> *And the way of it long*
> *I came out on the chariot of the*
> *First gleam of light*
> *And pursued my voyage through the wildernesses of worlds*
> *Leaving my track on many a star and planet*
> *It is the most distant course that comes nearest to thyself*
> *And that training is the most intricate which leads to the utter simplicity of a tune*
> *The traveler has to knock at every alien door to come to his own*
> *And one has to wander through all the outer worlds*
> *To reach the innermost shrine at the end*
> *My eyes strayed far and wide*
> *Before I shut them and said 'Here are thou !'*
> *The question and the cry "Oh where?'*
> *Melt into tears of a thousand streams*
> *And deluge the world with the flood of the assurance 'I am!'*

Does this poem bear any semblance to the stanza of Tapaswini on which we are focusing? The theme is not similar. Characters are also not the same. Then where is the similarity in both the couplets? If we go beyond the externalities and probe into the deeper meaning behind the words, we realize that they talk about the same inner

---

2 Poem No 12, Geetanjali, Macmillan & Co. 1912

experience. Rabindranath sets out as a traveler in search of the ultimate truth. In Tapaswini, Tamasa River is also a traveler spreading joy on the way, but her long journey is to reach the ultimate destination. Though river Tamasa doesn't express her desire, it is evident that she has been aspiring to embrace Devi Sita since her birth. She has been flowing, cascading, crossing many a mountain and forest only to get purified by the divine touch of Sita. Then is the God of Rabindranath the same as Sita? The answer is clear. Sita is the particle of the same divine element that Rabindranath experiences. Rabindranath travels round the universe but when he closes his eyes he sees God residing in his innermost crevices. Similarly after crisscrossing the entire land Tamasa River reaches her ultimate destination of finding Sita. Her quest ends there. When Rabindranath searches God with a fervent heart flooded with tears, God replies that I am within you, similarly Tamasa's earnest prayers are answered when she attains Sita and embraces her with an ardent fervour.

Rabindranath is the name of such a stream which has started its journey to its own inner self with a pure yearning and craving in his every breath. In Tapaswini, Gangadhar is 'Tamasa' who is longingly praying for the arrival of Sita. Gangadhar is also like Rabindranath, a pious stream whose name is Tamasa. With this insight if one peers into the poetic innards of both Rabindranath and Gangadhar, the mature readers can find both the poet's deep attraction to the divine beauty, divine light and divine potency that exists in the universe. With this appraisal it can be said that both the poets are similar on this aspect.

Rabindranath's heavenly soul music resonates in Geetanjali. And it is not that the poet was not having worldly cares and responsibilities. He was full of them.

Yet through all the mundane distractions he was conscious of the purpose of his life. Such pure consciousness was akin to the Vedic quest for meaning of life. It is worth mentioning that both Rabindranath and Gangadhar were the true inheritors of the Vedic tradition. The zest that was inherent in Rabindranath's life; the same spark was fully present in Gangadhar. The entire Geetanjali is a fountainhead of Rabindranath's inner spiritual calling. And in his poems they had found full expressions. Gangadhar instead had not expressed his life callings directly but had portrayed it through various characters and situations in his poems. Tapaswini would not have been special, if his life philosophy were not reflected therein. Simply to choose a subject and embellish it with words was not the intention of the poet. What Maharishi Valmiki, Sant Tulsi Das, Mahakabi Kalidas, Bhavabhuti or Balaram Das had not expressed, were brought out in the poem Tapaswini and those unique insights have enriched it. This is not to underrate the originality of any of the poets mentioned above, as each one of them was illustrious in their own brilliance. Gangadhar was only an inheritor of their tradition.

Rabindranath had repeated what the sages of Vedic tradition had recited many millennia before. Nevertheless Rabindranath is considered a shining beacon of originality and genius. Because what he expressed as the inheritor of Vedic tradition, was imbued with his own self realization that was unique to his creative efflorescence. If he had not mastered the Vedic soul of the Rishis and sages he could not have created such poetic exuberance in Geetanjali. Thus in the works of these two poets, the voice of the quest of our ancestors can be heard.

The discovery of his inner self had led Rabindranath

to have a vision of the Creator with the help of his inner eyes just as Arjun had seen with wonder and astonishment the Vishwaroopa of Lord Srikrishna in the battlefield. In being able to see God in his myriad ways rests the greatness of a poet. The path to sublime literature lies in transcending the external world and sublimating the inner stirrings. As with Rabindranath, it was with Gangadhar. Immersing himself in the pristine waters of River Tamasa he pined for Sita and like River Tamasa, he attained it. Gangadhar's description and Rabindranath's inner feelings are similar and special in their own ways. Therein lies the beauty and timelessness of Geetanjali and Tapaswini.

❑❑

Wives of Rabindranath and Gangadhar: Mrinalini and Shanta Devi

Maharshi Debendranath knew very well what a pure romantic soul his son Rabindranath was. The need to keep his temperament under a leash was felt by him and from such a wish a discovery of sorts happened. A small girl was selected as Rabindranath's bride. Her maiden name was Bhabatarini. At the age of ten she was given in marriage to Rabindranath who was then twenty two years old. Bhabatarini was illiterate at the time of marriage and her family status was no way comparable to the aristocracy of Tagore's family. Despite all these disparities, Rabindranath was not able to defy his father's wishes.

Rabindranath accepted her with one change; he changed Bhabatarini's name to Mrinalini. Mrinalini rhymed with Nalini, a woman in whom Rabindranath had a love interest in his teens. The romantic inclination from which father Debendranath wanted to lure away Rabindranath itself became a loop into which the child wife was drawn, being showered with her husband's affection , then a budding young poet.

Mrinalini too returned the poet's fondness with her commitment to him. She was the perfect foil to the poet's creative genius. She could keep him charmed with her tender care and attention so much so that soon Rabindranath's creativity flowered and spread its wings.

Under Rabindranath influence too unlettered Mrinalini became proficient in Bengali, Sanskrit and English. She even translated some portions of Mahabharat and Katha Upanishad to Bengali. She also acted in one of the dramas written and directed by Rabindranath which used to take place regularly at the Tagore family house. She had totally immersed herself in the life of her husband, thereby aiding in the making of a creative genius. She was always simply dressed and shorn of any ornaments. The couple had five children and Mrinalini took great pleasure in dressing them up as if her beauty was reflected in them.

But Providence had other plans for the loving couple. It is a mute question as to why artists go through such separation. After shifting to the new residence in Shantiniketan, Mrinalini fell grievously sick. She was brought to Calcutta for medical treatment. But Mrinalini could never return to Rabindra Sadan. On 23rd November 1902 she breathed her last leaving all grief struck.

During her sickness, Rabindranath got more close to her. He nursed her tenderly during those difficult times. In those days there were no electric fans. The poet used to hand-fan her day and night to give her a touch of cool breeze. The day she breathed her last, he did not allow anyone to come near her, but spent the last night looking at her face with tearful and loving eyes all by himself. His eyes were transfixed on her.

Rabindranath has portrayed a wide spectrum of emotions through his writings. In many of his poems, his love for his wife has found expressions in very tender ways. Lying down in bed with tired eyes welling with tears he has expressed his adoration for her in a very touching manner. In moving words he has prayed to the Almighty with a heavy heart, "The night has melted into early morning. You have embraced it extending your arms. I have come to you to dedicate all my offerings of love. Oh God! Girth of my house is very small. Whatever vanishes from here does not come back. Oh God! Your span is endless. I have come to your door hoping to find Mrinalini in your vast expanse."

While rummaging through the belongings of his wife, after her death, Rabindranath had discovered some letters addressed to him by Mrinalini. He treasured those letters as a prized souvenir till the end. Later he authored a collection of poems titled 'Remembrances'. Rabindranath did not marry again. Rest of his life, he spent reminiscing her memory.

While recollecting the love ballad of the poet and his muse, a parallel too can be found in the lovelorn life of Swabhav kabi Gangadhar.

Kabi Gangadhar's wife Shanta hailed from Remanda village of the present Bargarh district. Her entry into the poet's family as if ushered in the entry of the goddess of peace. She gave two sons and two daughters to Gangadhar. Amidst the task of bringing up the children and taking care of aged parents her mind remained steadfastly devoted to her poet husband. Though unlettered, she could fathom what is meant by a wholesome, upright life style of her husband, in full measure. Being illiterate like Mrinalini at the time of marriage but unlike her having no opportunity to be educated or desiring so, she was mature and sagacious enough to appreciate her husband's godly qualities. Sadly such an affectionate, warm and devoted-to-family soul was not to live longer. Who would have imagined that a calamity would befall the poet's close knit loving family? In those days sudden epidemics used to sweep villages and wipe out large sections of the population. The year was 1897, when the scourge cholera broke out in the village. People deserted their houses and took shelter in open spaces under the trees. Gangadhar along with wife Shanta and the extended family took shelter in the mango orchard of Rabanaguda village some three kms away from Barapalli for one week. Later the villagers allowed them to come into the village, but Shanta Devi suddenly took ill. Help of traditional healers were sought, but it was of no avail. In such tragic circumstances Shanta Devi breathed her last leaving the family completely shattered.

After the epidemic waned, Gangadhar returned to his village weighed down heavily by the loss of his beloved wife Shanta. The four children lost their loving mother and how they would have missed her in every moment of their life can only be imagined. Shanta's persona was so self effacing and gracious that even when she was able to speak a little in her last moments, she had requested the poet with tears in her eyes to marry again. This gesture is enough to speak of how caring she was towards her children and husband. Gangadhar's grief, if anyone could understand; were his four children. Just as their mother's doting words and tender care was unforgettable for them, Gangadhar's ears too kept reverberating with her sweet and adoring voice. She had never uttered an unkind word to anyone in her life time. No wonder he wrote:

Kete aparadha kari sakhi dine
Dekhi nahin toro mana
Dine to mukharu karkasha bachana

Pai nahin moro kana
Kalanadi bina garba kharba kara
Bachana na kahi pade
Galu nimajai dei sokamaya
Dustara ghoro birodhe

[1]*So often had I caused you offence dear*
But never had I found you sore,
Not for once did my ears receive
Harsh words from your lips, and now
In your voice that trounced the tinkling veena
You say no word to me
And have left me drowned n
Grief and fear, awful, insupportable.

There can be no comparison between Mrinalini and Shanta Devi. Rabindranath had written poems in memory of Mrinalini. Gangadhar had not done so. But while depicting Sita's character in his poem Tapaswini, he has relied on his own life experience; borrowing glimpses of Shanta Devi's character. Instead of directly expressing his personal loss he has very skillfully woven it into the pathos of Sita. Many critics concede that the inner beauty of Sita as portrayed in Tapaswini was inspired by the loving nature of Shanta Devi.

The creative souls of Rabindranath and Gangadhar were similar in many respects. The tragedies of life were faced by them with great fortitude and patience. Their faith in the Almighty was strong and unshakeable. While an ordinary mortal considered misfortunes as curses these souls with their divine ingenuity turned these adversities

---

1 Indumati:Translation by Soubhagya kumar Mishra; Gangadhar Meher: Selected works (2001), p 303

into blessings. As if they could establish subtle unions with their lost ones. With rare insight such sage like poets could penetrate the mysteries of this world's sufferings and see what lay beyond the obvious.

Both Mrinalini Devi and Shanta Devi had got married at a very early age. Both were ideal wives and mothers in their short lives and both were epitomes of woman-hood as glorified in Indian culture. In the Indian psyche, sacrifice rather than pleasure is the embodiment of God realization, which in the perspective of western civilization, may appear archaic. It is equally true that in the name of tradition and superstition women in India have suffered a great deal over the ages and social reformers have gone to great length to mitigate their sufferings. Notwithstanding the aberrations, the glory of Indian women is resplendent in the characters of Sita, Sabitri, Anusuya, Shakuntala - a fraction of that light sparkling in the lives of Mrinalini Devi and Shanta Devi - as well.

It appears that some souls take birth for a special purpose in this world and after that purpose is over they return to the other world. The lives of Rabindranath's and Gangadhar's respective muses - Mrinalini Devi and Shanta Devi - did serve such a purpose of inspiring both the poets to create immortal poems whose allure endures even now. To label them as only ideal house-wives or life partners would be belittling their substantial contribution to the inner consciousness of both the poets.

❑❑

The first poem of Geetanjali and Bharasa poem of Gangadhar

Rabindranath was a firm believer of divine blessings. The first poem of Geetanjali is a touching testimony to his total surrender to the Divine. That Rabindranath's own English translation of Geetanjali was in a separate creative league of its own is widely acknowledged by his critics. The same is too echoed by Haraprasad Das, a well known Odia poet while translating Geetanjali into Odia. He considers the poet's English version as an instance of distinct creative excellence. The first poem from that English translation is now compared with 'Bharasa' of Gangadhar Meher.

Who doesn't know of Rabindranath's inner voice; his capitulation to the divine? In his own words "this frail vessel thou emptiest again and again and fillest it ever with fresh life". Such is his faith that even when his vessel is emptied he considers it as a great blessing; because he knows it will again overflow with divine compassion. Human life is short and fragile. But when the Divine caresses, the benevolence of the Creator is felt by the perceptive heart. Rabindranath's sensibility was so drenched with joyfulness and divine ecstasy that his verses became an ode to spirituality. It was not that he was not beset with worldly tribulations. He had to face many challenges in his personal life. But amidst all ups and downs of life his inner self remained unruffled. When a person with tranquility offers all his devotion to the Supreme, the utterances of his soul are transformed into gems of celestial revelation. Such was the beauty of Rabindranath's poems. The music in his poems is heavenly as his heart strings produced unsurpassed melody. Time moves on relentlessly, but the heart of Rabindranath that is forever yearning for divine love, remains immersed in heavenly bliss for his faith goes beyond the vicissitudes of mortal life.

> [1]*The infinite gifts come to me*
> *Only on these very small hands of mine.*
> *Ages pass and still thou pourest,*
> *And still there is room to fill.*

Gangadhar also reposed such faith in the Supreme Being. His poem 'Bharasa' resonates with the faith in Almighty with the same intensity. He has the confidence that he will one day receive His benediction. God cannot keep any soul in misery for long. Days of despair pass, so do the gloomy nights. Finally when divine blessings start pouring in, the poet's heart overflows with joy. He writes,

> [2]*How can you spurn*
> *That which you yourself have made!*
> *Your punishment I'ld deem my glory -*
> *How then wouldn't you soften towards me?*

---

1 Geetanjali Macmaillan & Co. 1912 poem no 1

2 Translation by Tapas kumar Chakrabarty, Gangadhar Meher: Selected works (2001) Ed. Madhusudan Pati The safe Harbour p.389

Yes, redeem you may or destroy
You may surely do as you please,
And knowing that all be your wish
This my self'ld quietly bide his time.

What God has created, He cannot reject. This is the poet Gangadhar's inner feelings. Generally a human being thinks of God as his well-wisher. Even saint Aurobindo says; "If God has planned hell for him why should he aspire for heaven?" It shows that what is good or bad for man is a mystery which only God knows. Those who are God-surrendered do not hanker anything for themselves but repose their complete faith in the Almighty, believing that whatever happens to them is the will of God and hence embrace it with total acceptance. In this context, writer Manoj Das quotes one touching verse, written by one young poet which was discovered after her tragic untimely death:

[3]*Jetebele asiba mo*	*Whenever comes the*
Antima muhurta	*Last moment*
Setebele hebi nahin bhita	*Will not be terrified*
Karna mun jane	*As I know*
Tumari nispati sada	*His wish is*
Karuna sinchita.	*Mercy personified*

Similarly Gangadhar writes in the poem Bharasa:

[4]*A secret truth have I heard, O Lord,*
And continually do ponder-
However great the sin, you can't
Force one out of your world ever.

---

3 The Odia Poem quoted by Manoj Das

4 Gangadhar Meher: Selected works, ibid

It shows Gangadhar's unshakeable faith in the Almighty. It is neither exaggerated nor pretended. It flows straight from his heart like that of Rabindranath. The staunch faith in God is what marks the beauty of the poems of both Rabindranath and Gangadhar and suffuses it with an unsurpassed melody.

❑❑

Sons: Shamindra and Arjun

Shamindranath Tagore was the fifth and youngest son of Viswakabi Rabindranath Tagore. Born in December 1896 in Jorasanko Thakurbari, Shamindranath was a doted child. In the temperament and childhood of this son, Rabindranath looked for his own identity. The beauty of the son's face mirrored his own childhood. Needless to say he was adorable. But as misfortune would have it, at the tender age of six, Shamindranath lost his mother. After his mother's death he was brought to Shantiniketan by his father, where he was under the care of his paternal aunt, Rajalaxmi Devi. Rajalaxmi Devi used to be under the care of Rabindranath's wife Mrinalini during her life time, so much so that Mrinalini Devi became the reason for Rajalaxmi Devi's total devotion to Rabindranath's family.

Rabindranath had many dreams for Shamindranath. But all his dreams lay shattered with his untimely death. He lived only for 12 years, 11 months and 10 days. The way he contacted fever and died came as a terrible shock to Rabindranath. His melancholy was amplified by the fact that Shamindra was a music lover and a thinker. From a very young age his talents had come to the fore. When he sang in his mellifluous voice, the whole atmosphere used to get electrified with emotion. After his sudden demise, grief stricken Rabindranath took refuge in Shantiniketan, immersing himself in its daily routine and work schedule. Condolences poured in from all quarters. The poet however showed great fortitude and remained stoic. In his later years whenever he drew a character of any child in his literary works, it unmistakably carried the shade of Shamindra. In the play of 'Dakghar', the character of the young boy Amal reflected the charming imaginative nature of Shamindra. In the poems too, the memories of Mrinalini and Shamindra shine through.

Shamindra was only a ten year old child. But the letters that he had written to his father makes surprising reading. In a letter he writes; "I can't read English books. Not even Geography and History. Whenever it rains, I am inside the house. Flowers have not come in the rose plant. Kadamb flower has also not bloomed only bakul flowers have bloomed." This he had written from Bolpur. In 1907 he writes to his aunt Rajalaxmi Devi; "Didi Maa I have received your letter, but couldn't reply owing to exams. After long I have found some spare time. But again exams will start. How are you doing? I am fine." He writes to his elder sister Madhurilata and one of his teachers in which his writing style is evident. He mentions about the birthplace of medieval Bengali poet Chandi Das, indicating that he was interested in writers and poets. Letters have been exchanged between Shamindra and his elder brother Rathindranath. The latter expresses happiness over Shamindra learning Japanese language. Rathindranath himself could not learn the language. So learning a new language by his younger brother had thrilled him. He used to share with him the activities of Shantiniketan; "Here apart from meetings and seminars, talks are being arranged almost every week. I went for one such talk. In this place, life stories of famous people of the world are being collected." Such exchange of letters – the only means of communication in those days - with a ten year old brother shows the precocity of the child, Shamindra. What a tragedy for the father to have lost such a son forever.

In the Rabindra Bhavan museum at Shantiniketan, a notebook is preserved which is decorated with Shamindra's handwriting. On the top is written 'Bande Mataram'. Ten songs of Rabindranath's and four stanzas of one of his poems are inscribed and at the end of each is engraved the signature of Shamindranth Tagore. From this it is evident how connected Shamindra was to his father's poetic journey in his short life.

From Subodh Chandra Mazumdar's letter it is learnt about the extent of care that Rabindranath used to take of his son. How he faced the premature death of his beloved son can also be gleaned from his letter to his youngest son-in-law Nagendranath. He writes; "We have to embrace the sorrow that is inflicted upon us by the Almighty. When God bestows on us suffering, we have to accept it as a testimony to our forbearance and patience. The stronger the blow, the greater should be the capacity to accept."

Many eminent people had reminisced Shamindra after his passing away, like Rathindranath, Mira Devi, Alama Das, Bhupendranath Sanyal, Jatindranath Mukhopadhyaya, Arun Prakash Bandopadhya, Sudhakanta Raichowdhury, Artist Mukul Chandra Dey etc. They all have described how he used to keep singing till his last days, how melodious his voice was, how talented he was in acting in their words. Another mysterious aspect was the fact that Rabindranath could communicate with Shamindra through the medium of planchette.

A parallel to Rabindranath's personal tragedy can be seen in Gangadhar's premature loss of his eldest son Arjun as well. Like Rabindranath, Gangadhar had many dreams for his son. Arjun was very fair in complexion and was good at studies. Gangadhar could see his reflection in his son. After Arjun completed class IV in village Barapalli, Gangadhar had aranged for his stay at Sambalpur for education in English. Entrusting responsibility of his son on the Head Master of the Zilla School, Dasarathi Panigrahi he had rested assured. But Providence had other plans. Arjun fell sick within two months and all treatment was proving futile. Gangadhar got him back to Barapalli, where his health was restored. But on one midnight in the month of July he suddenly fell seriously ill. Arjun's younger brother Bhagaban along with their sister and bother-in-law were present at home while Gangadhar was away at Bijepur on work. Messengers were sent to get him back. On hearing the news Gangadhar rushed to Barapalli. It appeared as if Arjun was waiting for his father's arrival because as soon as he came, the father and son's eyes met, a subtle sentiment was exchanged and the son closed his eyes forever. Gangadhar was shattered. After his wife's death the sudden passing away of a beloved son was a great blow to him, more so, as he was a very affectionate child. At the time of death he was only 13 years old.

Arjun's affectionate nature had been recounted by the younger brother Bhagaban till he lived, and lived he did till the age of 86. In his book Pitru Prasanga he has recollected vividly his father's disconsolation at the premature death of Arjun.

At the time of death Arjun was already motherless

just as Shamindra was. Gangadhar had a special feeling for the motherless kids. He had taken upon himself both the role of Father and Mother. Loss of the child left him crestfallen. Many letters from Kabiguru Radhanath Ray, other fellow poets and well wishers poured in. They all commiserated with his personal tragedy and said that only time can heal his wounds. Such comforting words coming from fellow writers would have definitely consoled him and wiped his tears. On his own, with great patience and a stoic attitude he tried to come to terms with his loss. Surprisingly in his poem Indumati - written a few years before Arjun's death - the verses had a foreboding of death. He had written:

[1]*The lamp of life keeps burning in the body*
For the span that the given oil lasts;
When the oil of years is exhausted,
The flame is forever gone.
The Primal Being; the Creator, who is beyond all thought,
Alone has the right to supply the oil
He takes note of the karma of different creatures
And justly distributes the oil
Whoever is born into this world
Would certainly die someday or the other.
The all-devouring Time at every moment
Keeps swallowing lives.

Did he have a premonition of the impending death? Though at one level he was grief stricken, on another level his inner self was tuning into to the philosophical note of life's impermanency. With unstinted faith in the Almighty

---

1 Indumati;Translated by Soubhagya Kumar Mishra, Gangadhar Meher: Selected works (2001) P.307

he tried to reconcile with his personal loss and on a deeper level communicated with the departed soul though not through planchette as Rabindranath could.

Rabindranath's attitude on the loss of his beloved son Shamindra is worth a mention. To his son-in-law Nagendranath he had written;

"The way Shami died all of a sudden, many had requested me not to share the news with Rathindranath who was abroad during that time. But when God has inflicted that tragedy on us it has to be accepted with equanimity – whatever sorrow has befallen Rathindranath, he too has to face it squarely - hence I did not delay in sharing the news with him. If this tragedy has not given depth and breadth to his lifestyle than before, then that is unfortunate. When fate wreaks a mishap it has to be accepted unquestioningly". (Kabiputra Shami pg 45, 47)

It may be seen that both the poets did not break down as ordinary mortals do, but kept themselves calm and unruffled as they were ordained to accomplish greater things in life. They were not like glass to break into smithereens in the face of adversity but were like diamonds diffusing light despite misfortunes. Gangadhar could swallow the toxin and spread nectar justifying his name Gangadhar, he who holds the Ganga, the pure.

Both the poets embraced their sorrow unlike the common souls who get distressed beyond control and lose the zest for life. Rabindranath and Gangadhar in their heart of hearts knew that sorrow is a gift from the Almighty. They knew how to sublimate their personal loss and immerse themselves in creative pursuits. From the depths of despair sprung the sprouts of new creations which they nurtured. After Arjun's passing away Gangadhar immersed himself in reading of the Mahabharat, out of which was created the poem Kichak Badha. It was as if deceased Arjun was inspiring him to keep writing and creating immortal poems.

They say it is only adversity which chisels a person's character. More so for writers and poets who create gems from the fountain of creativity. Misfortune makes them more introspective, meditative and pensive out of which arises a new consciousness that is resplendent in its new trajectory. It was equally true for Rabindranath and Gangadhar.

❑❑

Poems: Bangamata and Matrubhumi

Viswakabi Rabindranath was the envoy of universal consciousness. Born in the leading aristocratic family of undivided Bengal he however, had not limited himself to any geographical boundaries. He had boundless love for his motherland Bengal. But at the same time, restricting the people of Bengal to the narrow confines of a region was anathema for him. From this point of view it is interesting to see how his world view was expounded in his famous poem 'Bangamata'.

Every person has an identity of his own. But he can move about in this world and he can transcend the narrow confines from the love of the place wherein he is born. That is the reason he had given a clarion call to the people of Bengal to first be a good human being. A mother always wants to keep her child next to her bosom, which is natural. Only when a mother's heart is stirred up for the world, then only she frees her children to step into the boundless path. Addressing the people born to the blessed land of Bengal, Rabindranath writes

[1]*In virtue or sin, joy or sorrow, rise or fall*
Make your child a man
Oh loving land of Bengal, in your lap
Don't keep the child bound forever
Wherever is the place for him
Let him find on his own.

Whoever eternally remains a child is devoid of world consciousness. This is not to say that the innocent pure heart of a child is not a desirable thing. What is being discussed here is that whosoever limits oneself only to its immediate surroundings, misses the growth of his inner self as implied by Rabindranath in the above lines.

In this context, a story comes to mind. Once there was a sage who used to move from village to village with his disciples. While travelling they came across a village where the inhabitants lacked minimum courtesy, good manners and honesty. While leaving the place he wished "May the residents always remain together in this place." When he moved to another village he was surprised to see all its residents with good conduct, good manners and honesty. While leaving the place he blessed them saying "you all inhabitants get dispersed." His disciples were surprised at such different blessings at two different places. The holy man explained what he meant by blessing differently; that those who are evil may not move out lest it spreads to other places and those who are good people may move so that their goodness spreads. His disciples understood the message behind his words.

In Rabindranath's call to the people of Bengal to travel beyond their homeland perhaps lay hidden this noble desire of spreading goodness. If those people of Bengal who adorn

---

1 Translation mine

their lives with love's myriad colours travel to different lands their great culture will spread. There may be another intention – to equally embrace the noble thoughts and good endeavours of other lands. Rabindranath always believed in give and take. He believed that life will be splendid if our fine aspects are integrated into western life style and the magnificence of western civilization is assimilated by us. No wonder Shantiniketan was a great meeting and melting point of the East and the West.

Rabindranath didn't favour keeping the children tied to their mother's apron strings. He wanted everyone's life to blossom through the trials and tribulations in the journey of life. Enthused as he was in a pan-Indian consciousness he didn't want his people to remain satisfied with only a Bengali identity. The remaining verses of Bangamata articulates this sentiment

[2]*At every step in small denials*
Don't keep him tied as a loving son
Bearing the hardships in his heart
Let him struggle with good and bad
If you don't keep all your weak, quiet sons
Out of your home and hearth
Oh Mother! Your seven crore children
Will only remain Bengali but not men!

The same message that is contained in the verses of Rabindranath resonates in Gangadhar's poem Matrubhumi in a very dignified way. The poet loved his birth place - the undivided district of Sambalpur - as much as the sacred land of Utkal. He was not confined to any narrow nationalism which is reflected in his poem

---

2 Free translation from Internet

Matrubhumi. The gradual development of the child's mentality is explained in very simple manner in this poem. His simple and evocative verses grant him the status of the best poet of Odisha and as a poet of world consciousness as well. When a small child goes to the neighbour's house he realizes that all kids are playing as him. When he moves from his neighbourhood to another neighbourhood his love expands. Then he loves his village which is so beautifully worded in Sachidanand Routray's famous poem 'Choto Moro Gaan ti' or Vinod Chandra Nayak's poem 'Grama Patha'. Gangadhar loved his village Barapalli dearly. In the last years of his life when he was insulted by the Zamindar of Barapalli many of his well wishers advised him to leave the place. But he refused to do so and worked for the amity between different sections of people of Barapalli. He loved Barapalli, he loved western Odisha, and he loved the entire land of Odisha and ultimately India. When a person extends his love of his mother land to the entire universe, his divine love is no way diminished. Gangadhar describes it in simple words

> [3]*Greater than heaven is the land that holds his home*
> *Grown wiser, when he appreciates*
> *The Master of the Universe is the father of all,*
> *He views himself as a brother*
> *To all mankind upon the earth.*
> *He then knows,*
> *The more the human beings one serves*
> *The more worthy does he grow as a son*
> *To the Master in His cosmic home.*

3 Translation by Chandrasekhar Rath, Motherland; Gangadhar Meher: Selected works p.377

When human knowledge transforms itself into love for the world it gets expressed in verses like that of Gangadhar's. The last lines of the poem are lovingly recollected by all Odias.

> [4]*If one in whose heart hasn't sprouted yet*
> *Love of the motherland and mother tongue,*
> *If such a one be counted among the wise*
> *Who then would be deemed as ignorant ones?*

Whenever we feel the surge of love for mother land Odisha and mother tongue Odia we sing this immortal couplet. The message that is enshrined in these lines stirs all hearts. From the small children to the adults and old alike, there is not a soul in Odisha who has not memorized these lines. That shows the power of Gangadhar's pen. Many other inspirational songs of Gangadhar is recited as welcome songs in many a meetings. For the first time the full Udbhodan song was recited some years back in the book launching ceremony of Germany- settled Odia writer Rajendra Narayan Das. Understanding of the poem will not only make someone a lover of western Odisha but also the entire Odisha and India. He will not only pass the test of narrow provincialism but get his sentiments elevated to love for Odisha and mother India. In another of his poem Iswardrohi he says whoever creates enmity between men detests God. With such words he has raised human consciousness to a spiritual level.

The similarity in the essence of both the poems Bangamata and Matrubhumi are striking. Rabindranath had gone beyond the shores of India. He had travelled abroad and had the opportunity to meet W. B. Yeats and Romain

---

4 ibid, p.378

Rolland, two giants of Western writers. Being proficient in English language he had translated Geetanjali into English which created a huge flutter in the Western literary circle. Gangadhar did not have any such opportunities. But his consciousness was at par with Rabindranath which is surprising. The poet who can hear his own subtle inner voice can only expand his consciousness with that of the universe and offer such immortal verses to his readers. It is the quality of elevated writers. They are certainly evolved souls. Rabindranath may be Viswa Kabi and Gangadhar Swabhaba Kabi, but both expressed the same noble sentiment in the epoch making poems Bangamata and Matrubhumi.

❑❑

Protests against British Rule

It is a misconception that Rabindranath was a supporter of British rule. It is said that the national anthem that was penned by him was in praise of the British rulers. It is true that he did not actively participate in the freedom movement. But he kept a hawk's eye on British government. His heart bled for the colonized, subjugated impoverished millions of Indians. He had accepted Knighthood from the British Government but that did not mean he had closed his eyes to the wrongdoings of British rule. The most horrific incidence that took place in Jallianwala Bagh of Punjab on Baisakhi day on 13th April 1919 shook his conscience. The news of hundreds of men and women falling like nine pins at the point of gunfire shot by General Dyer left a deep scar in him. His reaction to the brutality unleashed by British Government was reflected in his heart-rending letter of 31st May of the same year to Lord Chelmsford, the-then Viceroy. The same was published in The Statesman of 3rd June 1919. He wrote:

"The enormity of the measures taken by the Government in the Punjab for quelling some local disturbances has, with a rude shock revealed to our minds the helplessness of our positions as British subjects in

India. The disproportionate severity of the punishments inflicted upon the unfortunate people and the methods of carrying them out, we are convinced, are without parallel in the history of civilized governments, barring some conspicuous exceptions, recent and remote. Considering that such a treatment has been meted out to a population, disarmed and resourceless, by a power which has the most terrible efficient organization for destruction of human lives, we must strongly assert that it can claim no political expediency, far less moral justification."

Pained by the massacre which had stunned the people from all corners of the country he takes on the anguish unto himself. He wrote, "Knowing that our appeals have been in vain and that the passion of vengeance is blinding the nobler vision of statesmanship in our Government, which could so easily afford to be magnanimous as befitting its physical strength and moral tradition, the very least that I can do for my country is to take all consequences upon myself in giving voice to the protests of the millions of my countrymen, surprised into a dumb anguish of terror."

Relinquishing the special honour decorated on him he wrote, "The time has come when badges of honour make our shame glaring in the incongruous context of humiliation, and I for my part wish to stand, shorn of all special distinctions, by the side of those of my countrymen, who, for their so called insignificance are liable to suffer degradation not fit for human beings. These are the reasons which have painfully compelled me to ask your Excellency, with due reverence and regret, to relieve me of my title of Knighthood, which I had the honour to accept from His Majesty the king at the hands of your predecessor, for whose nobleness of heart I still entertain great admiration."

In Odisha there was no dearth of support and respect

for British rule. Swabhav Kabi Gangadhar never received any honour from the British Government nor did he hanker for it. For his poem 'Victoria Staba' he received brickbats. This was written towards the end of First World War. He wrote another poem titled 'Mahaprayana'. It was written on the event of death of King Albert Edward VII in 1910, who was then the King of the United Kingdom and the British Dominions. Writing such poems did not mean that his love for his countrymen was any less. Rather he was keen on Indians receiving benefits as much as possible from British rule. However later on when he realised that Indians are suffering from the ill effects of foreign rule he got disillusioned. In one letter to his friend Brajabandhu Panda he wrote "I am not craving to be in the service of any King. Can there be any king bigger than the British King? When I am disenchanted with the British Kings, why will I want to be in the service of any other king?" (Dated 28th September 1915; Gangadhar Granthabali pg 470)

It is true that he never lobbied with the rulers of the day. His poems Victoria Staba or Mahaprayan did not get him any monetary benefits. The kings described in his poems were all benign, magnanimous rulers. He was pained to see injustice meted out to the subjects by rulers. In the last stage of his life he protested fearlessly and peacefully against the highhandedness of the Barapalli Landlord. Just as he remonstrated against the young ruler of Barapalli, he voiced his protest against British rule which found expression in his poem Bharati Bhavana. Written in 1922, this poem was his last literary piece. Penned with British nib and paper but with self made ink, this composition poured out his angst against foreign rule.

Just as Jallianwala Bagh massacre wounded the heart of Rabindranath, it did the same to Gangadhar. Bharati

Bhavana reflected it in good measure. He did not get an opportunity to see Mahatma Gandhi from close quarters, but keeping track of the freedom movement from the news papers, he understood that Gandhi is the Godsend liberator of an enslaved India. The picture of Gandhiji that he had in his mind, had found eloquent expression in his poem Bharati Bhavana. The poem was written in such a way that two strand of ideas were depicted. On the surface, one was based on the Gopis and Krishna while the underlying one was against the torture of Indians in the hands of the British rulers. Some critics have questioned the fear of the poet Gangadhar in creating such a subterfuge. But it can be said that the plot was a ploy to mask his abhorrence to foreign rule. The patriots understood the real meaning of the poem just as revolutionaries wearing camouflage attacked the rulers.

In the first stanza Gangadhar writes:

[1]*In the empyrean of the Golak complained to the Lord the maiden Muse,*
All that you have done on the Indian soil the mind cannot efface;
O Lord of Gopa, you have defiled our class and clan by deceit
And on whatever was our own imposed your lordship

In masked words the poet says; Oh King It is not possible to forget what you have done to our country. You have used trickery and deception to destroy our self respect. You have wrested our independence from us'

---

1 Translation by Chandrasekhar Rath 'Musings of Mother Bharat', Gangdhar Meher: Selected Works(2001)Ed Madhusudan Pati p.384

In another stanza he writes:

[2]Akrura offered you worship and ignoring his pains to Gopa went
And, far away, you cared not for our anguished cries and lament;
The banner of fame fluttered the whole world over
That by skill you could douse all fire and so Ugrasena grew happier.

Here 'Akrura' stands for Mahatma Gandhi, 'fire' stands for General Dyer and the Amritsar massacre, 'Ugrasena' stands for British Parliament.

In words that conceal, Gangadhar says, 'After Gandhiji started his disobedience movement, your brutality and cruelty have been proved. You rewarded General Dyer who ordered the firing on hundreds of innocent and unarmed people of India. You have put Gandhiji in jail and all appeals and prayers to free incarcerated Gandhiji have fallen on your deaf ears.'

The verses from Bharati Bhavana used to be recited by Barapalli's freedom fighters - Bhagirathi Patnaik and his revolutionary son Prafulla Patnaik - to mobilize people against British rule and kindle nationalist fervor in them in those troubled times.

Gangadhar did not live to see the independence of India. Nor did Rabindranath. Gangadhar breathed his last in 1924, while Rabindranath in 1941. But their patriotic zeal expressed through their poems stirred the imagination of the people and created a groundswell of nationalist feelings that carried them through the freedom struggle.

2 ibid p.386

Shantiniketan and Barapalli

A highly conscious and creative person not only dreams for himself but always remains in a dreamland to create a beautiful world and a beautiful society for mankind. The dreams that Russian writer Leo Tolstoy saw for his village Yasnaya Polyana as described in his autobiography is well known to his readers. Mahatma Gandhi's dream for an egalitarian society was successfully experimented in his Ashram at Sabarmati. The dream of making Shantiniketan a centre for creativity was also successfully translated into reality by Vishwakabi Rabindranath which has proved to be a rare instance in this world. When the uninhabitated, desolate land belonging to his Father Maharshi Devendranath was inherited by Rabindranath, it was bereft of any human bustle or vegetation. On this Godforsaken land he created his place of worship. To build an institution of world repute, he gave all his body mind and soul. The new life that he breathed into Shantiniketan and the vivacity of Viswa-bharati University that he had set up has today made it a place of pilgrimage among India's educated mass. Shantiniketan was that educational institution where Rabindranath had sown the seeds of human values and human conscience. Today the seed has grown into a huge tree and has become one of the leading premier institutions of national importance in India. The whole world finds a beautiful nest here. It is a place where the East meets the West. Shantiniketan is the expression of Rabindranath's modern liberal and global thinking. Conferring degrees was not the main aim of this institution. The aim was to spread lofty human values. Today some of his dreams may have undergone changes, but the soothing and gentle ambience of the place transports each and every student, teacher and visitor- whoever goes there - to a world of peace that is simply difficult to describe.

The comparison between Rabindranath and Gangadhar's poem has now opened up. Both were successful poets of the same time. The spiritual calling in both the poets manifested in their poems bearing the beautiful signature of their hearts. Gangadhar's Arghyathali in Odisha is as popular as Rabindranath's Geetanjali. Many articles analyzing their creative genius can be written. But these two poets were not satisfied with only writing but went beyond their creative pen and wanted to create a beautiful world. Rabindranath's dream centre was Shantiniketan, while Gangadhar's dream village was his birthplace Barapalli.

The huge sacrifices that Rabindranath made to make Shantiniketan a verdant and lushly beautiful place was like him writing a long poem. The trees that he planted are still giving - to all those who visit the place - a cool shade a la Rabindranath. That, Shantniketan is the greatest living legacy of the great poet hardly needs any reiteration.

If we turn our attention to Barapalli a village of undivided Sambalpur, where Gangadhar Meher was born, we find that it was a large village, even in those times.

After spending his working life in Sambalpur, Bijepur and Padmapur, Gangadhar at the age of 58, had returned to his village with loads of dreams. But he did not have the freedom that Rabindranath had, for transforming Shantiniketan to an educational centre. Barapalli was being ruled by the village Zamindar. There was no dearth of narrow minded, self-centred people in the village those days. Still Gangadhar wanted to make an ideal village out of Barapalli. He even gave up his literary activities and instead devoted his time in bringing about cohesion and harmony between the disparate social groups. He set up an institution called 'Sadhu Samiti'. The objective of this organization was to bring about fellow feeling and establish peace and brotherhood amongst the warring factions of the village. After his return from Padmapur on retirement, he presided over many an organization in the village and therefore commanded respect and love from the people. He was also a well wisher of the ruling Zamindar family. But the arrogant son of the Barapalli Zamindar could not appreciate his large heartedness, noble and righteous spirit. The caste sentiments between different factions fanned by the young arrogant Zamindar and evil minded people stoked a fire of unrest in the village. Gangadhar tried his best to douse the caste conflagration with his virtuous words and action. In the face of life threats from the ruling family, he remained steadfast, courageous and well intentioned to unite the belligerent sections. At the fag-end of his life, he convened a conference of the Meher clan to remove the superstitions and make it a more civilized group. His efforts bore fruit but he couldn't live to see Barapalli as an ideal village free of evils. At the age of 62, four years after his retirement, in April 1924, he breathed his last. The last years of his life, were completely devoted for the welfare of his people in the village.

From this angle, Rabindranath was a successful idol of a successful play in Shantiniketan, while Gangadhar was a frustrated player in Barapalli's caste drama. There is absolutely no comparison between these two on this aspect. One was a successful institution-builder while the other was a failed social reformer. However, the dream that both the poets cherished to see was similar - a society free of superstitions, ignorance and the 'fragments of narrow domestic walls'. To the outer-eye Shantiniketan stands for eye-catching beauty while the inner eye only can see the Valmiki and Kanwa Muni's hermitage so beautifully envisioned by Gangadhar in his literary creations. Gangadhar's inner world was full of love, peace and harmony. That it could not be translated into this material world is our failure, not Gangadhar's. Just as Rabindranath's poems bring out the beauty of life and keeps inspiring generations after generations, so also the words of Gangadhar, immortalised in his poem 'Honeyed' inspire all Odia-speaking people with its immortal words

[1]*Look O life, honeyed is this universe*
Look how full of honey it is!
The stream of honey will erase
Your sins and mortal fears

New deeds, new meanings,
Ever new paths to knowledge,
Reveal on this earth in newer light
Countless streams of honey, O life!

---

1 Translated by Jayanta Mahapatra & Madhusudan Pati; Gangadhar Meher: Selected works (2001) p365

Two Prayer Poems

The first stanza of the first poem of Viswakabi Rabindranath is famous among the cognoscenti.

> *[1]O Lord! Help me bow my head under the dust of your feet*
> *O! Help me drown all my arrogance in my tears*

This couplet illustrates the way Rabindranath likes to surrender himself to the Almighty and has no parallel in the modern poetic tradition. It shows the poet's desire to wash away his vanity with tears of love for the Almighty. Such a poem emanating from his pen was possible because of the environment in which he grew up, the books that he was given to read, the company he was surrounded by and the Vedic tradition that he followed since childhood. If the heart is not soaked in divinity, if each nerve and sinew is not steeped in spirituality, such words will not flow from the pen. When genuine tears roll down the eyes, the heart gets cleansed of conceit and pride. It has famously happened with Viswakabi Rabindranath. The subsequent lines from the same poem elaborate his longing for surrender of the ego:

---

1 Translation mine

[2]In giving glory to myself I only debase myself
In being immersed in me, I only go around in circles
Help me drown all my arrogance in my tears
Let me not project myself in my work
Let your will be done in my life
I ask for your eternal peace,
in my heart your everlasting presence
Surround and shelter me in your lotus heart
Help me drown all my arrogance in my tears.

The poet says when a person is given to self praise and self glorification he only degrades himself. Similarly when he is absorbed in self advertisement he turns away from the divine. Only when he surrenders to the Omniscient and feels His omnipresence he realizes eternal peace. He invokes the protection of the Merciful. Such words sublimate the reader. The reader soaks in the beauty of these verses that opens up his mind and emancipates his heart.

The immortal prayer song that Rabindranath has given to his Bengali readers has a parallel in Gangadhar's oeuvre too. Gangadhar has given an immortal prayer song to the Odia readers in his anthology Arghyathali. The first song in the anthology is Bhakti which is sung across Odisha in all the schools. The first stanza of the song goes like this:

[3]O Lord, Life of the Universe,
Unwilling is my heart to call you
An Ocean of Mercy, for only a drop
Of your mercy makes the ocean.

To say that Gangadhar's Bhakti song is as popular

2 Translation by www.geetabitan.com
3 Adoration: Translation by Madhusudan Pati & Jayanta Mahapatra, GangadharMeher:Selected Works (2001)p.361

in Odisha as Rabindranath's first prayer song of Geetanjali will not be an exaggeration. For Gangadhar, it is not enough that we call God as an ocean of mercy for the ocean is a drop of His mercy. It is difficult to comprehend His mercy. In poetic terms, the poem was a brilliant composition. Like Rabindranath, Gangadhar wants to remain secure surrounded by His mercy but he goes a step further and unlike Rabindranath, he says God's mercy is incomprehensible. In the same song, he writes:

[4]*A drop from the ocean of nectar am I,*
Who had quit the sea and ascended the sky
Descending then, mingling with the nectar stream,
Should the heat of sin wither me on the way,
I shall turn into dew and come down again.

Rabindranath wants to go underneath the dust of God's feet, but Gangadhar says that he has no strength to bear the dust as millions of planets and stars have adorned the feet of God in the form of stardust.

[5]*You have not given me strength to bear*
The dust of your feet on my head
For countless suns roll
As dust at your feet

Outwardly Gangadhar's couplet appears in contrast to that of Rabindranath. While Rabindranath seeks the dust, Gangadhar says he doesn't have the capacity to absorb the divine dust. The enormity of the Universe which lies supplicant at God's feet is beyond human imagination

4 Ambrosial: ibid p 364

5 Adoration: ibid p 361

and a mortal like him doesn't have the strength to bear the stardust. Here, Gangadhar has surpassed Rabindranath in words though the underlying sentiment of both the poets is to submit before the Almighty. Both have derived divine peace and solace from their absolute submissions.

Gangadhar feels that he cannot establish God's image in his heart. Just as it is difficult to imagine the Himalayas in a seed of mustard so it is, to place the image of God in one's tiny heart.

> [6]*There is no space in my little heart*
> *To enshrine your image*
> *For how can the Himalayas lie*
> *In the womb of a mustard seed*

Rabindranath on the other hand implores that the magnificent and splendid beauty of God be enshrined in the lotus of his heart so that he derives lasting peace.

> [7]*I beseech your lasting bliss*
> *By keeping in my lotus heart*
> *Your matchless magnificence*
> *Securing eternal peace*

While Gangadhar finds it difficult to encapsulate the grand image of God in his heart, Rabindranath desires to place him in the lotus of his heart. A comparison of the two prayers shows the two poets in different light. One is awed by the incomprehensible presence of God while the other wants to place Him in his heart. The engagement with divinity is the same, only the expressions are different. In

---

6 ibid p 361

7 Translation mine

this context, the great Lebanese poet Khalil Gibran's words appear relevant. He writes: 'It is more logical to say that I reside in God's heart than God residing in my heart.' The way different poets express the same divine connection between man and God differently is a matter of their perception.

In the last stanza of the poem Bhakti, Gangadhar writes:

> [8]*That this ego is mine alone*
> *In no way can I disown,*
> *This, I offer from afar, O Emperor of the Universe*
> *As a gift at your sacred feet.*

The last word for both the poets is unconditional surrender to the Almighty. What Rabindranath has done so has Gangadhar. There is no contradiction, no limitation, no pretence, no ruse or maneuver in their devotional feeling. When the heart is absolutely clean and is bathed in love for God, the poems become sublime, uplifting and transcendental. Rabindranath and Gangadhar exhibit the same depth in their devotional songs, though their manner of expressions may have been different. Both have discarded the cloak of ego from their hearts and raised their hands in absolute surrender to the Almighty. It is the reason why the prayer songs are the first choice for recital in Odisha and Bengal. Children are made to recite the songs to lift the veil of arrogance and conceit. Both the prayer songs are like steady beacons in dark clouds of ignorance.

❑❑

---

8 Translation by Madhusudan Pati & Jayanta Mahapatra, Gangadhar Meher: Selected Works (2001)p.362

Invoking the Divine and Celebrating Amrut

If Rabindranath's Geetanjali was soaked in divine sensibilities, Gangadhar's poems were drenched in divine nectar as well. At the time Rabindranath was being decorated with the Nobel Prize in 1913, Gangadhar's pen was quite active. He was a regular reader of newspapers and Bengali magazines and periodicals. So it is improbable to think that he would not have read the good news of the Nobel Prize being conferred on Rabindranath. Equally he would not have been deprived of reading his writings in Bengali as well. Both the poets were not known to each other and Gangadhar had not mentioned Rabindranath anywhere in his writings, but it is unlikely that he was ignorant of such a genius.

It is surprising to see the similarity between Rabindranath and Gangadhar's writings. It cannot be conclusively proved that Rabindranath had influenced Gangadhar. But their thought process and poetic sensibilities produced similar poetic outpourings. One was a poet in Bengali language, another a poet in Odia language. Their consciousness produced the same resonance which reflected in their writings. There are poems of both the poets which reverberate with the same flavor. In the famous song, 'Tumi naba naba rupe eso prane' Rabindranath writes:

[1]*Come to me in ever new forms varied and various*
In fragrances, colours and songs
Come to my limbs with a touch delightful
To my heart with joy eternal
To my closed two eyes with fascination
Come to me in ever new forms varied and various

In simple words in the song Rabindranath's soul is inviting the Almighty, which is intelligible to all. There are no complexities, no intricacies no verbosities, nor any perplex thoughts in the song. The poet is praying to the Almighty to manifest himself in different forms, in the form of aroma in flowers, in the form of colours, in the form of songs. When he comes in varied ways life becomes supremely fulfilled. That divine touch the poet craves for can be seen by him even with closed eyes. In the second part of the song the poet writes:

[2]*O' pure and radiant glow*
With even destinies strange
Come in my joys and sorrows,
In all the mysteries, in daily chores
Even when all activities end
Come to me in forms, varied and various

God descends where there is purity, clarity and soulfulness. That is why the poet exults in the divine in the form of truth, consciousness and joyfulness. Amidst all

1 Translation www.geetabitan.com
2 ibid

the daily chores, in the thick of joys and sorrows, the poet wants to experience the beauty of God.

After reading this poem let us divert our attention to Gangadhar. Gangadhar too expresses divinity in his scintillating verses. He sees the world as an expression of God's 'honeyed sweetness'. In his poem Amrutamay (Ambrosial) he writes:

> [3]*The fragrance of newly opened buds*
> *The rhythm of new verse delicious*
> *The melodious call of birds in the wild*
> *The flowing music of children's prattle*
> *The forest of blissful virgin clouds*
> *And the tender face of the newborn child*
>
> *Ambrosia all… all flowing nectar*
> *Carries away life in ecstatic flow*

In the second stanza of the poem it is expressed even more lyrically. Gangadhar sees the touch of the Divine in every beautiful scene, in every melody, in every blooming flower. He waxes lyrical seeing the splendid nature around him. In the gentle breath of the cool breeze, in the moon beams of milk white gossamer, in the soft drizzle of rains, in the delicate light of dawn and in the dew on the green grass; everywhere Gangadhar sees the ever-flowing honeyed sweetness of God that enthralls all.

In the third stanza he writes:

> [4]*The twinkle and glimmer of stars,*
> *The drip drip of falling rain,*

---

3 Translation by Jayanta Mahapatra and Madhusudan Pati, Gangadhar Meher: Selected works(2001)p363

4 ibid

The sun charging forward to dispel the murk
The exulting earth from darkness freed,
And the sounds of waterfalls leaping along:

Ambrosia all, all flowing nectar,
Drenches this life to bliss

The song of Rabindranath welcoming the Divine to his life in all forms and Gangadhar's celebration of the honeyed sweetness in every visage of nature in his song Amrutamay

invoke the same divinity. Rabindranath's song imbues the reader's heart with a pure and divine feeling while Gangadhar's poem Amrurtamay opens the reader's eye to the presence of divine all around in nature and the universe. The beauty that is inherent in both the poems springs from the same spiritual consciousness of both the poets. Their language may be different, their birth place and upbringing may be different, the social milieu in which they lived may have been different, but their moral and spiritual predilections were very similar about which there cannot be two opinions.

❑❑

Fighting Adversity

Human life is a parable of obstacles, sorrows and misery. Sorrow is a universal experience. However, rich, strong or powerful a person may be, he is not free from adversities in this mortal world. Hence fear of adversity is a natural emotion. When a person becomes helpless, scorched by obstacles and hardships, he turns to the Almighty to rescue him from the misfortunes. He pleads, prays in desperation, in extreme despondency to spare him the mental anguish and sinks into despair.

Only those who are composed and face happiness and sorrow, pleasure and pain with equanimity remain unperturbed. They are unruffled because of their unwavering faith in Almighty. They show remarkable patience and forbearance in face of adversity. To the common man such examples are a source of strength and inspiration. When mauled by misfortune a person prays desperately for divine mercy. At his weakest moment if someone can instill in him mental strength and fortitude, it is a saint. Rabindranath was such a saint poet who wrote poems on adversity;

[1]*This is my prayer to Thee*
My Lord - strike, strike at the root of penury in my heart
Give me the strength lightly to bear my joys and sorrows
Give me the strength to make my love fulfill in service
Give me the strength never to disown the poor
Or bend my knees before insolent mind
Give me the strength to raise my mind high above daily trifles
And give me the strength to surrender my strength
To thy will with love

This one stanza of Rabindranath is enough to infuse mental strength in a person deep in adversity. It inspires him to nurture a deep faith in the Almighty despite the turbulence in his life. Even if he is bereft of sympathy and help from his fellow human beings, he need not lose his bearings, for the mental strength he prays for will help him tide over the trials and tribulations of life. The poet espouses readers not to waver in one's faith in the Supreme Being for therein lies the mystery of adversity. A great poet like Rabindranath exhorts the readers to face the joys and sorrows of life with equanimity and not to lose their faith in God. In the poem, he urges that despite storms in life one should not cease one's love for God. He does not ask God to remove his troubles, but to give him enough strength to face the troubles.

Like Viswakabi Rabindranath, Swabhav kabi Gangadhar too espouses the same sentiment among his readers. His poem on adversity is unique in the sense that he writes from the view point of Almighty instead of the devotee:

---

1 Verse 36, Getanjali, Macmilan & Co. 1912

[2]*The king of beasts with his animal nature*
Might kill off his subject, the deer,
But how should I, a god,
Perform such an unholy, cruel deed?
That one being god should destroy his dependents -
This is utterly unheard of and never seen:
If I exterminate those in my keeping,
Why should then the earth's people adore me?
After they come to know,
The humans were intent upon the death of ***bighnas,***
The later are wreaking their vengeance on men.
But those who befriend them and with cordiality please
The ***bighnas*** *give them courage and make them happy,*
Revealing the path to success.
The ***bighnas*** *are ever the guardians*
Keeping watch over my storehouse of success –
Success that never comes within the grasp of those
Who keep away from them in fear.

In this poem, Bighnaraj (Lord Ganesh) says that the obstacles and hardship that lie in the path to success and happiness is a test to the strength and courage of human beings. He assures that being the remover of obstacles he cannot leave his ardent devotees in misfortune forever. He is aware of their hardships. The *bighnas* (obstacles) are designed by Him only to test the faith of men in the Supreme power. If they pass the test they can taste success. Writing from the vantage point of God, the poet has thus revealed the secret behind the sorrow, pain, dangers and hurdles that befall every human being on this earth in a very ingenious way. Instead of being discouraged and daunted, he says, men must try all means to overcome them

2 Translation of Ganeshankara Atmakatha by Chandrasekhar Rath Gangadhar Meher: Selected Works, p. 372

with full faith in the Supreme Being. He instills tremendous strength in people to rise above the impediments, because at the end success awaits them. The obstacles are meant not to dampen our spirits but to trounce them and eventually taste happiness. Understanding of this truth is what makes the evolved souls lead a fearless life while reposing their faith in Almighty.

Similarly in Rabindranath's poem there is no prayer to shield one from adversities but a loving exhortation to conquer them. This world is not a straight line. Human life is bedeviled with sorrow, anguish, anxieties and pain. But buckling under them and remaining agitated is not the way, rather facing them squarely with patience and grit is the path to eventual success. In critical times it is easy to lose faith in the Supreme Being, but the words of poets, philosophers, sages and the wise restore our faith and trust in God. Their words guide us like a beacon of light in the darkness of adversities. They are the treasures of our society and civilization.

Rabindranath and Gangadhar, though belonging to diverse backgrounds have expounded the same truth. Both the writers have been able to create the same emotion of divine love and unflinching spiritual faith in the hearts of the readers. That is why they are held n the highest regard by men and women, the young and old in fact by all categories of people at all times. Their poems are like guiding lode-stars in the terra firma of human experience.

❑❑

Study in Ideation

Rabindranath's Prose 'Ramayan'& 'Shakuntala' Gangadhar's Poem 'Tapaswini' & Pranay Ballari

Mahakabi Valmiki's Ramayan and Mahakabi Kalidas' Abhigyan Shakuntalam had a great impact on both Rabindranath and Gangadhar. What Rabindranath has encapsulated in his two small prose pieces on the two epics, Gangadhar has elaborated the same theme in his two poems. Whether it be prose or poem the similarity in their ideation amazes the readers. The culture of India is reflected in Ramayan and Abhigyan Shakuntalam. So how could Rabindranath, the creator par excellence not take cognizance of them? So was the case of Gangadhar. He too embodied all that is in India's civilisational values and made it the subject matter for his poetic works. A study of their works reveals their convergence in assessing the two epics.

Rabindranath in his prose piece titled 'Ramayan' contains some very significant points. This piece was written as a foreword to Dinesh Chandra Sen's 'Ramayan Katha'. Elsewhere he writes, "There are a category of poets in whose writings a whole land, a whole age expresses its feelings, experiences and makes it eternal in man's consciousness" (Nibandhamala p.355) The characters; Sri Ram, Lakshman has kept the entire population of India in an emotional bonding for thousands of years. He writes; "The specialty of Ramayan is that the story of a family is magnificently magnified. The relation between father and son, between brother and brother, between husband and wife, the righteousness, devotion between each other has been glorified in such a manner that it becomes the stuff of a great epic. The fidelity of a son to his father, the sacrifice of a brother for another, the faithfulness between the husband and wife, the pledge of a king towards his subject can go to what extent has been delineated in Ramayan" (Nibandhamala p.358)

What Rabindranath felt about the characters in Ramayan, Gangadhar felt the same: the embodiment of sacrifice and fortitude as shown by Sita is the theme of his epic poem Tapaswini. What Gangadhar has portrayed in Tapaswini is certainly immortal. In Tapaswini, Sita's enormity of sacrifice has also been equally matched by showing the egalitarian aspect of Rama's public character. The emotional bonding between husband and wife and their sympathetic understanding of each other for the sake of their subjects has made Tapaswini stand out in a league of its own. The character that was vilified in Ayodhya is portrayed as the purest soul, the queen of hearts by Mother Nature. This is the height of Gangadhar's creativity for which Tapaswini has reached the pinnacle of success. It is true that Tapaswsini's reach is limited to Odisha. That the verses of Tapaswini have reached every corner of Odisha needs no reiteration and the fact that it is in the lips of all Odias of all generations is a testimony to its immense popularity.

In Tapaswini Sita glorifies the character of Ramachandra in the following verse:

[1]*Whatever be the torments that strike the heart*
From your mouth flows only a sweet nectar

Similarly the appeaser-ruler SriRam is described by Gangadhar in the following verse:

[2]*Lightning's fire scorch its heart, yet the cloud must rain,*
Renouncing al joys the king must please his subjects,
And so be worshipped high

The characters, SriRam, Lakshman, Bharat, Satrughna, Valmiki, Anukampa; all the inhabitants of the hermitage as portrayed by the poet move the readers.

Rabindranath also expresses the same sentiment. His last lines on Ramayan, "The empathy, the kinship, the honesty, the faithfulness, allegiance and dedication all that is shown in this epic saga, if one can accept it heartily, it will bring in the fresh air of the ocean into the small windows of our habitats" (Nibandhamala p.361). This shows his appraisal of the characters.

Gangadhar had penned the epic poem Pranay Ballari, inspired by Abhigyan Shakuntalam, while Rabindranath wrote a prose piece titled Shakuntala as a literary review. Rabindranath writes "In Abhigyan Shakuntalam, the meeting of heaven and earth has been easily accomplished by Kalidas. He has turned fruits out of flowers and extended the earth into the horizon of heavens, so much so that no one can observe the distance between them". (Nibandhamala p. 363)

Rabindranath had also compared Kalidas' drama with Shakespeare's Tempest but what he was searching

1 Translation by Jayanta Mahapatra & Madhusudan Pati in Ganagad har Meher: Selected Works (2001) p.11

2 ibid p.27

for was; nature as a character. In his words "In Abhigyan Shakuntalam, Nature is a character just as Anusuya, Priyambada, Kanwa and Dushmanta" (Nibandhamala pg379). This is exactly how Gangadhar has portrayed Nature in both of his poems; Tapaswini and Pranay Ballari. In Tapaswini mother nature glorifies the character of Sita while in Pranay Ballari, nature becomes an ally of Shakuntala.

Gangadhar has even gone a step further. He could not shatter the innocent heart of Shakuntala by Dushmanta's betrayal. The twist is that he depicted Shakuntala as a naïve maiden, construing the betrayal as a prank played by Dushmanta on her. Gangadhar believed that the trust that is once broken between husband and wife is difficult to restore, hence he has characterized Shakuntala as a candid, simple hearted and love-struck maiden in his poem.

Shakuntala's lament has also torn the poet heart of Rabindranath. He draws the attention of the readers to the pathos, simplicity, patience and forgiveness that plays out in the drama and elevates his appraisal to German poet, Goethe's voice and writes "Following Goethe's critique, I reiterate that the rhapsody of youth in the beginning of the play Abhigyan Shakuntalam transports earth to heaven at the end" (Nibandhamala p. 378)

Rabindranath's literary criticism of Kalidas finds an echo in the depiction of characters in Gangadhar's Pranay Ballari. What Rabindranath had tried to establish in his literary criticisms of Ramayan and Abhigyan Shaknutalam, Gangadhar has interpreted it in the same way through the characters in Tapaswini and Pranay Ballari. At the end one can conclude that Gangadhar's insight of beauty was similar to Rabindranath's consciousness of beauty in all that was beautiful in the mind's eyes of the two poets.

❑❑

Drishtidan and Tapaswini

Geetanjali may have earned Rabindranath the coveted Nobel prize and given him the epithet of kabiguru, but it is common knowledge that he had a large corpus of other forms of literary work such as short stories, novels and dramas as well. He has almost 100 short stories to his credit. Most of his stories were women centric, portraying their struggles, turmoils as they existed in the Indian society during the late 19th century and early decades of 20th century. His short stories have received wide acclaim, included n text books for children and adult alike, translated on celluloid and remained in the best selling anthologies of short stories, worldwide.

One such heart touching story of Rabindranath is Drishtidaan. The story of Drishtidaan has an uncanny similarity with the theme of Tapaswini. Both the themes are women centric. Tapaswini is awash with the pathos of Devi Sita, who is supposedly banished to the forest by the people of Ayodhya. She takes refuge in the ashram of Valmiki and is indulged by the Ashram inmates and the sage Valmiki who shower her with love and affection. She learns about the Aswamedha sacrifice being done by her husband, Raja

Ramchandra at Ayodhya. For the ceremony, she knew, the king has to take a consort which is part of the royal custom. This thought agitates her mind and she writes a letter to her husband Ramachandra. The letter is replete with feelings of a rejected wife, her insecurities, her attraction for her husband and the undying love she cherishes in her heart for him. In depicting these emotions Gangadhar shows exceptional understanding of female psychology. Sita Devi is not annoyed with her husband for taking a second wife, but would like to know the virtues of the woman for whom he has taken a fancy.

In Gangadhar's words Sita writes in her letter

[1]*The one who is worthy today of your embrace*
What arduous penances had she done in the past,
Where, and how long, and what mantras did she chant-
This alone, my Lord, kindly let me know,
For I have no need of any other wealth
To me that would be far more precious

After writing the letter, Sita comes to know that the king Ramachandra has not married for the second time. Rather the king has placed a golden statue of Sita at the prayer hall. This is conveyed to her by her two dear twins Luv and Kush who are witness to the royal ceremony. After hearing this news, Sita Devi's heart undergoes a change for her husband and she rues her wanton emotions. She seeks apology from her husband for being weak hearted and harbouring such baseless thoughts while he has always been the epitome of unwavering love and sacrifice.

---

1 Canto XI, Tapaswini ,Gangadhar Meher : Selected works (2001) by Jayanta Mahapatra and Madhusudan Pati p 93

In Gangadhar's words Sita exclaims:

[2]*'Oh I am the ever sinner,*
Writing words that would have scorched my master's heart!
I am a frail woman, weak within,
But deep and boundless is my Lord's compassion
Forgive my wrongs, my Lord, Ocean of Mercy
Destiny has made me your heart's poison'

Now let us come to the Drishtidan story of Rabindranath. In the story, the hero is a doctor, who fails to give timely medical treatment to his wife, as a result of which she becomes blind. Despite this tragedy befalling the couple, their mutual love and affection for each other remains undiminished. To this world of the engrossed couple enters a third person; a woman by the name; Hemangini. The suspicion of the blind wife that her doctor husband may take Hemangini as his wife creates a tempest in her heart. To add fuel to her inner fire, a relative praises Hemangini's beauty and qualities. Unperturbed the blind wife however, welcomes Hemangini to her household and never lets her love for her husband be tarnished by a second woman's presence, whom she cannot see but can only sense. When she comes to know from the relative, that Hemangini's marriage is certain, her composure wavers, she pleads before her husband and questions him as to what is wrong with her. The doctor husband clarifies that he needs a woman and not a super woman and then leaves the house in a fit to Hemangini's house, whereupon the wife falls unconscious.

In the last scene, when the wife opens her eyes she finds herself in the lap of Hemangini, who asks her what

---

2 ibid p 95

is wrong if she gets married. The wife instantly blesses Hemangini not knowing whom she is marrying. Soon she finds out that she is marrying her brother and not her doctor husband as feared by her.

The name of the doctor's wife is Kusu. When Kusu discovers that Hemangini is not marrying her husband but her brother, an avalanche of emotions drenches her. When her husband comes to her in the night and proclaims her as his goddess, she smilingly says she is his wife, only an ordinary woman and has no intentions to become a goddess or super woman. How the Doctor averts getting into a second marriage, however, remains a mystery in the story.

The character of Sita portrayed by Gangadhar would appear a few notches higher than Kusu. Sita prays to her husband Ramchandra to share with her the noble traits and sacrifices of his newly wedded wife. Kusu too indulges the other woman Hemangini and feels that her blindness is the reason for her husband fancying another woman. When she comes to know that Hemangini is not marrying her husband but another man, her heart is filled with terrible remorse and she sheds copious tears for harbouring suspicion against her faithful husband.

If one examines minutely, Kusu's character is an extension of Sita. Both Rabindranath and Gangadhar were experts in understanding women psychology. Drishtidaan story is written in first person. Rabindranath has written the entire story imagining himself as Kusu. Gangadhar too has poured out Sita's inner churnings putting himself in the place of Sita. One is a prose piece and the other a poem. One is a classic epic saga of ancient India and the other a social episode of emerging modern India. But in both the creations, the interplay of love and resentment of both the female characters are depicted in the same tender manner.

Rabindranath was the master of Bengali language, while Gangadhar was that of Odia. Rabindranath was born in 1861, while Gangadhar's birth year was 1862. Both were great litterateurs of two adjoining states during the same time period. In both their writings, one may be prose and one poem, the women-centric theme is evident. But their women centrism was of a different flavor. Sita Devi's devotion to her husband Ramchandra was legendary while Kusu's devotion to her doctor husband is exceptional if not equal to Devi Sita. So their feminism was expressed in their genteel remonstrations and questioning of their fate. They did not submit to their fate unquestioningly but wanted to know the reason thereof.

Drishtidaan of Rabindranath is not a very short story. It runs into twenty three pages and while reading gives the feeling of a long poem. If Gangadhar's Tapaswini can be translated into Bengali it can give the readers a scope to assess the similarities between the two creations. Tapaswini has been translated into English, Hindi and Sanskrit but not into Bengali, a language which has more affinity with Odia language.

It is the responsibility of the critics, translators and litterateurs of Odisha to get Tapaswini translated into Bengali and give the Bengali readers a comparative flavour of the women-centric theme of both the celebrated writers; Gangadhar and Rabindranath.

❑❑

Two Ideal sons

If keeping oneself behind the scenes and completely dedicating one's life to establish the fame of one's father can be considered a creative pursuit, then the sons; Rathindranath Tagore and Bhagaban Meher will get the credit hands down.

Just as Rathindranath was inspired by his father; Rabindranath's idealism, Bhagaban Meher too was indoctrinated by his father; Gangadhar Meher. Bhagaban never worshipped the God Goddesses as much as he did his father. Mother Shanta Devi did give him birth, but the rebirth he got for the second and third time was by his father Gangadhar. In his younger days he had fallen sick and was bedridden for a considerable length of time. His mother Shanta Devi by that time had passed away. Gangadhar looked after him like a father would, with the tender touch of a mother's love. His complete dedication to his ailing son and earnest prayers helped Bhagaban to recover. He also took the help of an Ayurved doctor whose medicines miraculously restored Bhagaban's health and vigour. Recovering from the jaws of death, Bhagaban repaid his gratitude to his father by assisting him in his work.

Viswakabi Rabindranath's son Rathindra had inherited the artistic virtuosity of his father in good measure. It was as if the creator had send to the family a perfect foil to match the genius of father Rabindranath.

Rathindra was a student of science. But he had a poetic bent of mind. His temperament was inclined towards arts and literature. His main passion was to studiously go through the corpus of Rabindranath's output. And what a copious output the poet produced! The letters exchanged between the father and son educates and inspires the readers till date. Rathindra played a major role in maintaining the peace and sanctity of Shantiniketan. Each tree, each building, each room, each flora and fauna in Shantiniketan spoke of Viswakabi's vision, in the making of which Rathindra had a major contribution.

Examining the life of Gangadhar and Bhagaban one can see the similar bonding. Though the father and son did not speak much between themselves or exchange voluble letters, they had a silent communion going on between them. Gangadhar had written a few letters to son Bhagaban, but they were neither descriptive nor advise-ridden. They were short and concise, but the underlying was suffused with father-son sentiment. Unlike the correspondence between Rabindranath and Rathindra's it did not have the voluble fulsome tone.

Gangadhar had lofty dreams for his village Barapalli. He had post retirement plans of working towards making it an ideal village in which Bhagaban had given his full moral support. But the events as, they unfolded, turned out to be hostile to him. Still he turned every crisis into an opportunity and created a Sadhu Samiti appealing to the nobler instincts of man. Despite the royal intrigues and narrow sectarian attitude of different groups in the village, he did not lose faith in the inherent goodness of people. He appealed to their higher instincts through his organization Sadhu Samiti and called upon the people to shun internecine enmity and work for the greater good. It is highly unfortunate that in those days, people of Barapalli could not fathom his noble and selfless attitude. Neglected, sidelined and for want of proper medical care he breathed his last, four years after he had returned to his village. After his demise, the whole responsibility of Sadhu Samiti fell on Bhagaban. People of Barapalli eventually realised the saintliness of Gangadhar and called upon Bhagaban to lead many a forum to propagate Gangadhar's values. Bhagaban in his unobtrusive ways provided leadership and carried on the mantle of Gangadhar almost silently. If one is asked who is the maker of modern Barapalli the answer would be the father and son duo. Barapalli got a new life after the death of Gangadhar, thanks to the efforts of Bhagaban in carrying out the unfulfilled dreams of his father. It was similar to Rathindra keeping the ideals of Shantiniketan alive after the death of Rabindranath.

Though a writer, Rathindra had not achieved much literary acclaim. But he was imbued with the beauty-worship of his illustrious father. The wonderful sketches and paintings that Rabindranath drew in the last phase of his life were coloured from Rathindra's palette. Many of his paintings adorned Shantiniketan. He served Viswa Bharati in many capacities, as horticulturist, teacher, administrator and curator of Rabindranath Tagore memorial and archives.

Similarly, the organizational capabilities which were latent in Gangadhar, found full expression in Bhagaban's personality. That social organizations can be free from egoism and pride, was exemplified in Bhagaban's attitude. Just as Rathindra dedicated himself to his father's unfinished work, Bhagaban also threw himself whole heartedly into his father's organizational legacy. Behind all the work that was done to preserve Gangadhar's legacy, there was one person's thoughtful planning and unstinted work. And that was Bhagaban's. He gave shape to the people's dream of keeping Gangadhar's memory alive. Making of Gangadhar's memorial, constructing his commemorative bust, converting his birth place to a public monument; all were possible due to his indefatigable work and whole hearted commitment.

Rathindra was not a writer but he had penned 'Pitrusmruti' in Bengali. The golden moments that he had spent with his illustrious father has been faithfully described in the book. Rathindra was equally proficient in Bengali too as Rabindrnath was. In English Rathindra wrote the book 'On the Edges of Time' reminiscing the memories of his father in exquisite English. Manoj Das, eminent Odia writer extolling the book, rued that such a book did not see a second edition.

Bhagaban Meher had exhibited his talent in writing poetry. However for writing prose, he got inspiration from Odia writers; Dr Mayadhar Mansingh and Gyanpeeth award winner Gopinath Mohanty. Their prodding resulted in his writing 'Pitru Prasanga', an honest biography of his illustrious father. This was written towards the fag-end of his life, the publication of which he was not fortunate enough to see. The same was translated into English after almost four decades. It can be said in all fairness that Pitrusmriti and Pitru Prasanga are two literary gems in the genre of biographies. Both Rathindra and Bhagaban had paid their gratitude to their respective famous fathers in their requiem, which clubs them in one club.

❑❑

Views on Education

Viswakabi Rabindranath's vision on education is quite well known to the world. Every teacher and student worth their salt knows how ground-breaking his concepts on education were. His Shantiniketan was an unconventional experiment in education. He took bold and courageous steps to seed and nurture the creativity, latent in every student. Such an endeavor of Viswakabi has not only been applauded all over the world but given him the epithet of Viswaguru (World teacher).

Rabindranath was aware of the problems and ills of conventional education. He had put all his efforts in bringing reforms in education. From primary education to higher education, all stages were discussed by him. That freedom is essential in the field of education was his constant refrain.

During his time, 'spare the rod and spoil the child' was the norm and teachers were unsparing with the hapless children. Rabindranath was of the view that such a strictly disciplinarian attitude will not help develop the child's personality. In this context he wrote, "Just as large space is required for moving about freely, without which health and happiness is affected, similarly in education a large space needs to be provided. If education is kept limited to the basics only, the mind of the child will not be enhanced. With essential education, some amount of freedom has to be given to expand the horizon of the child's mind and make him a better person. Without freedom and with age, the child will then not grow and his mind will remain stunted."

Rabindranath vociferously advocated education through mother tongue. In his view education through mother tongue is the best way for mental development He opposed the view that all mental thoughts and heart's language cannot effectively be captured by mother tongue. Rather he said that it is only through mother tongue that a child can speak his mind and heart freely. His view is relevant even today. Not able to write a letter in mother tongue, not speaking in mother tongue with one's own friends or disrespecting the books written in mother tongue are the terrible sins according to Rabindranath. These were indeed remarkable opinions coming from Rabindranath, the champion of liberal education.

Rabindranath had dreams of how the students' life should be scripted. His vision behind setting up Shantiniketan way back in 1901 was not only a compelling idea but an incredibly marvelous one to which the world sat up and noticed. To start with the basics he wanted his school to be away from the crowded locality. Ideally it should be in a secluded place where under the sky, amidst the greenery and the open spaces, the school will become like a hermitage. In such a serene environment the teachers, professors can immerse themselves peacefully in their research and studies. Gurudev's idea on education was to transcend all man-made boundaries. Keeping this vision in mind, if one observes the multilingual, multicultural institution of Shantiniketan, it can be said that it is a dream actualized in full measure.

So much has been written and discussed on Rabindranath's ideas on education, which is certainly commendable. From this angle if we analyse the ideas of Gangadhar on education, we have to delve into his poetry more than his prose. Students have scrutinised his thoughts on education intrinsic in his poems and have even obtained PhD degrees, which is heartening. Students have probed into his writings and dug out his views on education, which is a matter of pride. His prose piece 'The educated, the uneducated and the educated-proud' contains his views on education. If one evaluates the piece one gets a fair idea of what he meant by the actually educated and the difference with the uneducated.

Describing the greatness of an educated person, Gangadhar writes, "The educated are true human beings. When the educated person does noble work and keeps the company of the virtuous and leads a life of a pious and righteous person, he can be called as truly educated." Such people are always concerned about the good of the society and the world at large. Their conduct resonates with the compassion of the Almighty. Their hearts are full of divine sentiments such as love, forgiveness and compassion.

What we understand by education and its definition, we can see it in the writings of Gangadhar. He writes "Education doesn't end in a school or college, it is a lifelong pursuit. The world is a school and nature is a book to be read daily". That there is no end to obtaining knowledge is realized by the learned and the scholars. An inclination towards literature is the hallmark of such educated and erudite persons. Among the educated such people are more precious than diamonds. Their hearts are like sky-kissing mountains, expansive and deep like the sea. Rising beyond the temptations of power and pelf, they are illuminated by their knowledge. In very few words, the way he has described the characteristics of the genuinely educated and their mental traits is certainly a gem of a prose piece.

Who to define as uneducated is also explained in this article of Gangadhar. According to him, an uneducated person is like an animal. He is engrossed only in eating and sleeping. In his conduct and speech he only exhibits his lack of character. Negative qualities like lust and anger makes his life meaningless.

Gangadhar could have stopped at describing the traits of the educated and uneducated and the difference between the two. But he has gone one step ahead and talked about a middle category whom he calls the educated-proud, which is little rare. These proud-educated appear to be doing good work, but their duplicity, deceit and craftiness gets exposed all the same. They project themselves as knowledgeable whereas they are always reluctant to gain knowledge. They bootlick those who are powerful and in good official position for their selfish interests.

Lies, deception, selfishness and pretense make their mind hellish though outwardly they appear honest and truthful. The rapid spread of such a category of the educated pollutes the society. To have observed such a tendency while writing this piece in the first decade of the previous century shows the futuristic insight of Gangadhar. For the educated it is an eye-opener and inspirational.

The copious discussions and articles on education that lies to the credit of Rabindranath are certainly missing from Gangadhar's opus. However his writings urging all to renounce narrowness, deceit and guile and striving towards humanism contains his message and is relevant for all ages to come. How big a book one writes is not the reflection of one's talent, but the substantive point one makes in one's brief writing is deserving of praise. In his lone article Gangadhar makes a wholesome argument in favour of right education as much as Rabindaranth has made albeit in a prolific way.

❑❑

Black Eagle Books

www.blackeaglebooks.org
info@blackeaglebooks.org

Black Eagle Books, an independent publisher, was founded as a nonprofit organization in April, 2019. It is our mission to connect and engage the Indian diaspora and the world at large with the best of works of world literature published on a collaborative platform, with special emphasis on foregrounding Contemporary Classics and New Writing.

www.ingramcontent.com/pod-product-compliance
Lightning Source LLC
Chambersburg PA
CBHW050426110726
47899CB00008B/2873

* 9 7 8 1 6 4 5 6 0 5 7 0 6 *